The NEXT STEP

WORKBOOK

Exercises in
Gratitude, Forgiveness and Action

TODD WEBER

Seattle, Washington

Published by Glen Abbey Books, Inc.

Cover design by
    Graphiti Associates, Inc.
    Seattle, Washington

This title has been bound using state-of-the-art **OtaBind®** technol-
ogy, which allows the book to lie flat.

First Edition
ISBN 0-934125-26-0
Printed in the United States of America

———————————————

10 9 8 7 6 5 4 3 2 1

For the Trinity Group,
For the ebb and flow that molded and shaped ...
With Love

Contents

Acknowledgment

Thanks to the Workgroup and all my clients for the acceptance and willingness to be my teachers; Bill Pittman, Linda McClelland, and Kelly Pensell for all the wonderful editing, artwork, and education; my homegroup, S.O.S., and Terry for being there all this time; my friend Wolf for help when it counted; and my family, for all the lessons learned. Special thanks to Edith, my mentor, for all her support and help.

Introduction

This book came about through an insight and awareness that was granted to me. I had been searching for years for a path that led directly to an awareness of God or a Higher Power and to unlimited growth and expansion. I was looking for a way to expand what I was gaining in a Twelve Step program and move with it and beyond it.

I tried so many different methods: lots of meditation, prayer, gurus, teachers, masters, and much, much more. I read and studied for years. I searched and searched. Being involved in recovery and a Twelve Step group was a great start, but it didn't answer all my needs. As I outlined in *The Next Step*, the companion book to this one, there is more to "emotional sobriety" than going to meetings and staying abstinent.

Then, through a series of seemingly unrelated events, I was thrust into an awareness and experience of creation and the flow of God's love. I had had glimpses of this feeling and experience in my deepest meditations, and an intuitive knowledge of it from "knowing" when I was an infant, before I was educated and taught.

This awareness and "knowledge" had always been there. I had just lost it, somehow. Now I know how to get it back and how to move into and stay in it more and more. It came to me through the practice of gratitude.

Gratitude affects every area of life. All the issues of self-esteem, prosperity, lack, spiritual growth, will, unconditional love, forgiveness, fear, irritations, and many others (including the areas most commonly associated with addiction recovery, ACOA, codependency, and "Child Within" concepts) are addressed directly by gratitude. It is so overwhelming, simple, and delightful that it is hard to accept as legitimate at first. I suggest you read through this book quickly the first time, then come back and go through it slowly, practicing the exercises as you go.

I developed these exercises and concepts further with groups of people who met with me regularly for a number of months, and with my workshop participants. Their experiences with the information and exercises convinced me of the validity of the practices and that it can be taught. It has developed into my purpose to share this fantastic chance for growth with others. Please approach this with an open mind and heart. It can stand alone or be used in conjunction with any religion, recovery program, spiritual path, or psychological plan for growth. It is not meant to take the place of any other belief or teaching. It is not meant to replace working the Twelve Steps. It is for use *with* the Steps to move into more growth and change.

The act of becoming is made of many parts. I will be discussing a few of them that have made a difference in my life. For a more in-depth look at the issues discussed here, *The Next Step* deals more with explanation and understanding. If that is your orientation, it will be a valuable guide. This workbook is about doing the exercises and learning *from* the experience. It is for *action*!

The main parts of becoming more "emotionally sober" are forgiveness (of self and others), gratitude, and action. Of the three, gratitude is the greatest, and simplest, gift.

Gratitude is the direct path to the heart and to a Higher Power. It is a means and an end, a method and an attitude. We will be discussing gratitude in many different contexts. It is so important that I cannot overstate how much we need to practice it.

Many other things are part of growing, but gratitude opens all the doors wider and more easily. Without gratitude, there can be no unconditional love, no total acceptance and appreciation of self. Without gratitude, there is no way to stay in the present. We are lost without it.

Gratitude

*Doing the gratitude exercise has greatly
enhanced my life. I'm more appreciative of all my blessings; clearer and
happier with my life. I don't seem to
have to analyze or ask why of anything
anymore and I feel very much at peace.*
—*Workshop participant*

*I'm seeing and feeling things for the
first time, again. I also remember these
experiences from my very early days.
When I listen to music I not only listen
to the melody, I also hear the individual
instruments. I'm more excited about
each day and feel so much more alive.*
—*Workshop participant*

Gratitude begins with the most basic things.
When a person is feeling the least grateful, that is when
it is most important to be able to see the good in a
situation or person. In order to move away from feeling
and being less than we want, and becoming more that
we do want, we must be grateful now.

It can be as simple as starting tomorrow morning by
being grateful for waking up. Start with the body: I am
grateful for breath. I am grateful for sight. I am grateful
for hearing. I am grateful for touch. I am grateful for

taste. I am grateful for food, and clothes, and shelter, and weather, and flowers, and bees. All make the miracle of life and all are now. Gratitude makes it impossible to escape into the future or back to the past. It forces us to be here!

When we become grateful enough, we blend totally into the flow of things. There is no more separation between "me" and "other." We are part of it all. We know without knowing and sense without senses. We become a part of the truth flowing directly from the Source.

The "flow" I refer to has many names and spiritual concepts associated with it. It could be called Samadhi, Sartori, bliss, the Void, and many other names. The current psychological term of "flow" refers to peak experience. I am talking about a larger concept. Flow includes an awareness of our cosmic connections—no separation, in awareness or fact, from the essence of creation and the power of the Source. Many contemplatives and spiritual paths have tried to describe it for ages. It is that place of the "unitive experience," where all is connected, creation and time are within as well as without, and love, as the presence of God, is the matrix of existence. It cannot be put into words. It is the experience of the majestic mystery of life.

Gratitude opens the gate of life, without reservation. With gratitude, abundance is not an issue. Of course there is enough—plenty! More than enough, of everything. Gratitude is a magic lens that shifts the perspective of the world to love and plenty.

Achieving an attitude of gratitude is not always easy. For some, it may take a lot of work and time, but

I promise you, if you become grateful it will change your life! You will *have* more, *be* more, *give* more than you ever dreamed possible. It starts with a simple exercise.

Every morning, for a month, get up a little earlier than usual. Get a pen and a piece of paper and write a list of the blessings in your life for which you have gratitude: family, friends, pets, God, breath, experiences you've learned from, lessons you've learned, and so on. Every day write out the list and you will be amazed at the difference in your life. Do it! Every day, for a month.

We will be adding to exercises done in the morning, but for now, just do the blessings list. (See the Worksheet at the end of this chapter.)

Now, it is not always possible to keep an attitude of gratitude. Life is not always easy, and we have a tendency to view things from a short-term perspective. It is difficult to see the good in abuse. It is very hard to be grateful for pain or to accept suffering. Many issues life gives us to deal with are tough. However, if we are persistent in looking for the good and working on gratitude, the necessary lessons are learned, the gifts revealed, and we move on.

Gratitude takes us ultimately to that place where we are in touch with our Higher Power. It is beyond imagination and concept. It is beyond most language. It is that place where the knowing and the being are one. As we become more and more grateful, we have more and more contact with that flow, and it gets fuller and deeper as we progress.

It is not a matter of technique or dogma. It is a matter of desire and heart. There is no right or wrong way to approach becoming more. There may be ways that will not serve you as well as others. Try not to think too much. Do the exercises, and let your action help your growth. Try to hear with the heart and move forward with faith and grace. This is a bountiful universe full of beauty and plenty. It is ours for the receiving.

The process of gratitude allows us to get in contact with what has always been there. When we were children, before words and judgment, we were constantly in the flow with God and grace. There was no knowing or not knowing—there was just the now. Becoming grateful allows us to touch a little piece of that flow—that connection with the Higher Self and God.

The Higher Self is a concept from Psychosynthesis that I prefer to use. It has similarities with the "Self" of yoga and the "Spirit" or "Soul" in Christianity. Many other spiritual paths have similar concepts. In Psychosynthesis, a spiritual awareness is coupled with psychological concepts to form a more balanced person. The Higher Self is that part of us that is connected to God, or the Source, and that has all the attributes of that higher wisdom. Incorporated in the Higher Self are the qualities of unconditional love, forgiveness, warmth, acceptance, compassion, charity, grace, openness, awareness, light, humor, and so on. We will discuss the Higher Self more in the section on forgiveness.

Just that little contact with the Higher Self, through gratitude, draws us closer and deeper. Soon we are able to direct ourselves into the flow at will. Staying in that state is not always easy, but it gets easier and easier to get back to it and to maintain it with the practice of gratitude.

Think about and practice gratitude every chance you get. Insights will flow continually. The medium of the stuff of life will become apparent to you. What we have always been becomes obvious—and life changes.

What a marvelous gift all of us have received. It is not exclusive. Anyone who can become grateful can become aware of the flow and gift of life.

We will discuss ways to make it easier and more direct, but it doesn't take a master to initiate you or some special technique or spiritual practice. It is there for us all, any time we can become grateful enough.

Do your list of blessings every day. It will change daily as you experience and grow. As we go deeper into the practice of gratitude, more becomes apparent for which we can be grateful, and life gives us yet more.

There is total abundance and joy in gratitude. It is just a small discipline to practice. Once you give it a try (an honest try—at least two weeks, every day, and preferably a month) you will not give it up. Life shares its secrets and unveils the keys to knowledge. It is spectacular and overwhelming. There is a tendency to draw back and question whether you deserve this bounty. Of course you do! (We discuss deserving later and in *The Next Step*.)

God gave each of us equal value in presenting the gift of life. We are all here with the same material to work with: grief and opportunity, sickness and health, success and failure. Sure, we have different talents and potentials, but we all have the same inherent value, and God, through the universe and its laws, makes sure we have equal opportunity to experience it all. Whether we live **Big** or not is up to us.

My challenge to you is: **Live Big!** Go for it all. There is no reason why we all can't share the abundance available, if we are grateful enough.

The practice of gratitude also has another benefit. With gratitude, one is able to look for and find the good in any situation. The ability to see the lesson or the experience for what is gained is priceless.

By being able to detach from painful or uncomfortable situations or relationships, and to see the benefit of the strength gained or experience gathered is tremendous. Detachment is a hallmark of balanced individuals. Gratitude gives us detachment without judgment or negativity. An experience just is, and the gift is in the lesson or experience gained!

 **Blessings Worksheet**

I am grateful for

Family:

Friends:

Neighbors:

Co-workers:

Teachers and mentors:

Experiences that were good:

Experiences that taught me:

Experiences that gave to others:

Insights and intuition:

Books, education, etc.:

Hard times, for perspective:

Health and well being:

Illness and pain, that taught me:

Beauty and joy:

Contact with God and the bounty of the Universe:

Recovery, sponsors, etc.:

And much, much more:

Irritations

In doing my irritation exercises, I found that they still have power until I take full responsibility for the action and realize and be grateful for the lesson. Then they go away completely. The result is that I feel lighter and more at ease.

—Workshop participant

Irritations, in the form of anger, frustration, fear, disgust, blame, etc., are one of the main barriers to gratitude.

I practiced movement therapy for a while. I was truly amazed at what the body held to itself. In posture, breath, fat, muscle tension, we literally hold (incorporate) our emotions. Little hurts and frustrations, long after we have forgotten them, are held in the body.

The mass of these hurts, angers, frustrations, irritations can literally "weigh" us down with fat or other body issues. Since it is all tied into self-esteem, it becomes apparent that gratitude is a self-esteem issue.

Gratitude, forgiveness, and those things that hinder them are all subjects that complement a Twelve Step recovery path. Dealing with these issues deepens and strengthens emotional sobriety.

Little hurts add up and clog up the pathway for growth and spiritual expansion. Here is a very simple exercise to add to the daily gratitude list that can clear these up quickly. You can literally feel the weight lifted from your shoulders.

Make a list consisting of little hurts, irritations, angers, and frustrations as far back as you can remember. If you can remember it, you can be sure your body does. This list is not for the major injuries like divorces, parents, siblings, or any other long-term incidents. (We will be discussing specific forgiveness exercises for those later.) This list is for naming and releasing the small stuff that has added up over the years and impedes our ability to feel gratitude. It should include the small things you may have "held against yourself" over the years. (See examples and Irritation Worksheet at the end of this chapter.)

After listing each incident, write a statement of release or letting go. At first, the feelings may seem to intensify, but soon afterwards, there comes a sense of release or completion after each statement. At that point, it is okay to let that statement go. As we start to get clear on some of these hurts and frustrations we've been holding, new ones will crop up that we've been holding at a deeper level.

This is very good. We can be thankful for the process and add the benefits of this exercise to our gratitude list. This exercise lets us move into our current body. We no longer have to hold onto the hurts and injuries of the past. Of course, we haven't covered all the big ones yet, but the cumulative effect of the little hurts can be overwhelming.

We release these small hurts. We no longer have to buffer ourselves against the pain with fat or bulk. We no longer have to hide the little child inside who is so sensitive to criticism and rejection. We no longer have to indulge in bingeing or overeating or drinking or drugs to dull the pain and create the person who deserves the hurt, rejection, and irritation that we feel.

We can be free to be who we really are: a deserving child of God, created with equal opportunity to partake of the bounty of the universe. We are big enough to let go of the hurt and release the pain. We have so much in our lives to be thankful for that we can release the small hurts (after acknowledging the lesson) and move on.

Even if you do not believe in God, it is widely accepted that there is a "collective unconscious" or "Source" that we can tap into. If you are having trouble releasing the small hurts and irritations, then tap into your connection with your Higher Self or Source and ask for help. Ask for the ability or motivation necessary to be able to let go of past hurt and injury.

Gratitude will take you to that Source faster than anything else. We will be discussing meditation and prayer later, giving a few methods that have worked for me in gaining direct access to higher intelligence and power. For now, use a sincere desire to let go of injury, hurt, and irritation that limits your ability to be grateful. However you appeal to your Higher Self or Source will be appropriate.

This is a different approach than doing a Fourth Step inventory. We are taking a look at those incidents that hurt, angered, or irritated us; times that we felt an injustice was done; times when life was unfair, when we felt helpless or hopeless to change something that needed changing. We will gradually gain a new perspective on accountability for those feelings, but for now, all we need to do is bring them to awareness and release them.

I am not asking you to take what I am saying on faith. I want you to try it and see how it works for you. This is not a doctrine or dogma. This program is not for followers.

Question it, analyze it, and dissect it—*after* you have tried it honestly, with good effort, for a month. Don't just read it and judge it based on its simplicity. Stop auditing life and live it!

Try these exercises and see what happens. I am willing to bet you will be totally surprised and delighted. If you are not, what have you lost? Probably a lot less than you will have gained!

 ## Irritation Worksheet

EXAMPLES:

Tommy sitting on my stomach
in grade school and
making me cry.   I can release that

Candi trying to knife me
when I teased her when I
was drying dishes.   I can release that

Peeing on Mrs. Faulkner's
carpet when I was 3.   I can release that

**Irritation, frustration,
anger, or hurt**   **Release**

1.

2.

3.

4.

5.

6.

7.

8.

9.

10.

Humility

*Learning to see the needs of others from
a higher perspective has changed my
whole view on service. I can be effective
now. It is very powerful.*
                    —Workshop participant

In the Twelve Step programs, humility is mentioned in the Seventh Step. I am talking about humility in a different way—an active, dynamic attitude of humility.

In the context I'm using it, humility may have a different meaning than you've used in the past. I define humility as the ability to set aside ego interests for the interests of the Higher Self and those of another person. It allows one to open oneself to the presence and availability of a higher and truer wisdom. Humility is being able to see the value in an answer provided through the Higher Self, even though it may not coincide with our beliefs or "truth."

This concept of humility is based on the Essene Law of Attitudes, as found in the Dead Sea Scrolls. The Law of Attitudes, in part, states, "A transpersonal attitude is theirs, those who see the needs of others *as they see them or will see them*, and fulfill them if practical."

Notice how this definition differs from the "Golden Rule" in that we seek to help others as *they* see how they need help, not how we might want to be helped in a similar situation. The perspective is much different. It is humble.

At the end of this chapter is an exercise that demonstrates our ability to connect with our Higher Self to humbly seek help for others or ourselves. This exercise is a genuine demonstration of the power of humility and of the innate wisdom of our Higher Self, which is always available to us. The practice and concept of humility is a fast, practical way to get in touch with our Higher Self. By learning to do this exercise, we become aware that the Higher Self uses symbols, feelings, and code, as well as language, to communicate with us.

In doing the exercise, trust the first response that comes to you. Don't second-guess or wait for something that "makes sense." Remember, the Higher Self is operating from a plane of infinite wisdom and knowledge, love, compassion, and grace. What doesn't make sense to you may make perfect sense to the person you are seeking to help.

I was in a workshop where we divided up to do a similar humility exercise. We got into groups, decided who would present a problem first, and the order of response from the others. We all made contact with our Higher Selves by becoming still inside and identifying with qualities of the Higher Self: love, wisdom, compassion, knowledge, strength, light, humor, etc. When the person presented her problem to the group, the first thing that came into my mind was a red balloon. It made no sense to me, and had no connection at all with the problem, but when I gave the symbol of the red balloon to the woman with the problem, it was a marvelous reminder of a solution she had forgotten. The balloon spoke directly to her and provided the spark for finding a solution. If I had judged my response based on what I "knew," I never would have given her the symbol. The Higher Self obviously had access to information I didn't (directly), and provided great help. By humbly accepting what was offered, everybody benefitted. Humility at its best!

In our workshops, we do this exercise in groups of three and always have a great time with it. The symbols and words received in humility *always* help with the issue presented.

To sum up: For now we are doing the blessings list daily, the irritations list and release daily, and the humility exercise once a week. If you feel this is too much—relax. Take what you can and leave the rest. One exercise at a time or many—it is up to you.

Our gratitude is growing daily for and from the lessons and experiences we are given.

 ## Humility Exercise

Take a few minutes to become quiet and receptive. Think of the qualities of your Higher Self and identify with those attributes: openness, acceptance, grace, forgiveness, humor, light, warmth, compassion, love, strength.

From this place of higher wisdom, think of a problem or issue facing a friend or family member. Think of the problem in very simple, direct terms, like "money," "job," or "daughter." Let that word or two represent the issue.

Go to your Higher Self and ask for a symbol or word that will help that person resolve the issue *"as they see it"*! Accept the first thing that pops into your mind. Write it down or sketch the symbol.

The next time you see that person, explain that you were thinking about them and their problem, and you received a word or symbol as a possible help to them. Offer it as a gift with no strings. I think you will be amazed at the results.

 **Humility Worksheet**

Person I want to help	Issue or Problem	Symbol or Word
1.		
2.		
3.		
4.		

The Will

Nothing can resist a human will that will stake even its existence on the extent of its purpose.

—Disraeli

This is an intense exercise! I have an uncanny feeling that my life is simplifying and resolving as I write. Feels like the baseline deserve level is rising. I see it in my thoughts about myself and what I see is possible to have in my life, amazingly, quickly, and effortlessly.

—Workshop participant

Until one is committed, there is hesitancy, the chance to draw back, always ineffectiveness concerning all acts of initiative and creation. ... [T]he moment one commits oneself, then providence moves too. All sorts of things occur to help one that would never otherwise have occurred .... Whatever you can do, or dream you can, begin it. Boldness has genius, power, and magic in it. Begin it now.

—Goethe

I **am** *really deserving—that idea is growing!! and this is opening me up to attract and receive more.*
                    —Workshop participant

The will may be the greatest gift we have been given. Just being able to say "I will" means we have a choice. We can choose to be different than we are. We can choose to stay the same. We can choose the direction we are taking and *move* that way.

Having free will means we can take action. What a tremendous ability! God has given us the means, on this level, to make things happen. The will is the instrument that ties our intellect and ego to the flow of creation and the Higher Self. We choose when and how to move into the flow, by an act of will.

The will is the instrument through which decisions are made. It is also the instrument through which surrender is made. People who are indecisive or "weak willed" have removed themselves from contact with and responsibility for their actions. It is all "out there," because, of course, acknowledging the will means we have to be accountable for everything. What an awesome responsibility! What a tremendous and grand gift!

We use the will all the time and usually are not conscious of it. We are not always aware of why we make choices or the motivation behind the choices. Learning the proper use of the will and developing accountability requires practice and a new perspective on some old concepts.

Attitudes and goals are uses of the will that we manufacture to filter information going into and out of the intellect.   Goals are specific targets which influence behavior and perspective.   Goals are only as effective as the focus and motivation behind them.

Attitudes are general lenses of belief that color our perspective of everything. We choose directly the attitudes and goals we have, and we see, hear, feel, touch, taste, smell, think, perceive everything through the filters of those attitudes and goals.

We have the responsibility for the way in which we perceive everything, and the ability to change it. We are not "stuck" with childhood beliefs or perspectives. We are not trapped by education or culture. We are only imprisoned by the bars in our heads. The spiritual masters have known for ages that a man is totally free as long as he chooses freedom. Putting people in a cell does not hold them.

We tend to think with the filters in place and only see through tinted glasses. When we choose to take off the glasses, my God, what a world! We get to see the whole panorama of life through the flow, and no filter can ever again dim the experience. If we choose gratitude!

The highest use of will is to choose to move toward God: to choose willingness, surrender, gratitude. The bounty and glory and freedom of the universe becomes apparent. The use of the will for goals and affirmations, prayer and meditation, aligning the intellect with the flow, are all powerful means of discovering purpose.

For it is only through purpose that true motivation, power, and passion in life can be released. Purpose gives focus for the will to work. Purpose propels one into the future with grace and dignity and plenty, giving to all in abundance and disdaining conditions. Living with a passion, moving toward a compelling future, being absolutely and totally in the now are all received from a purpose. Using the will to stoke the engine of that purpose makes the fulfillment of its meaning irresistible.

It is so hard to contain the excitement and energy released when a person puts the will behind a noble purpose. Mahatma Gandhi had a noble purpose with a will. Jesus had a noble purpose with a tremendous will. Mohammed had a noble purpose with a fiery will.

All great leaders, industrialists, and prophets had a great purpose with their total will behind it. It cannot be stopped. It is undefeatable. Failure does not hold it down. Low self-esteem is swept aside before it. Poverty is defenseless against it. God himself opens the door to the universe for the person with a noble purpose and the will to make it happen.

So, what is your noble purpose? What is your passion? What is it, when you dream, given no limitations, that you would endeavor? What would you fight and die for? Where is your heart and soul hidden?

Does a noble purpose need to be "huge"? I don't think so. Victor Frankl's *Man's Search for Meaning* gives us an idea about purpose and its scope, or take a look at some of the work of Dennis Waitley, Ph.D. Both have worked with and defined purpose very well, and provided a perspective in which to place it. (See the companion book to this one, *The Next Step*, for further discussion.)

Being a great parent can be a noble purpose. Being a "good" parent doesn't quite ring the same bell. "Being an embodiment of my faith" can be a noble purpose. Being a "good member of my church" doesn't quite catch the same passion. A purpose is not a half-way thing. It is a way of living that you can dive into head first, and take things as they lay while you work your will to become the product of your purpose.

Who do you want to be? That is the real question. Do you know who it is that you are and will to become? "When I grow up I'm going to be....?" Not only a function, but a being! It doesn't matter *what* I do for a living, it is *how* I do it that counts. As long as it is within the universal laws and my own code (doesn't harm others, etc.), then it is the *style*, as well as the content, of how I live that counts.

What has my *being* on this planet meant? Will I leave a message by my living that can be read by others so that they benefit from it? Is the message in the saying or the living of it? Am I proud of the message of my life? Are you?

Once again, I challenge you to live BIG! Don't settle for less than you can be. Live totally, no holding back, without limits!

Let's take a few minutes to get our purpose in focus. Sit quietly, breathing softly and slowly. Let your body relax. Let your mind go soft. No clinging to ideas. No holding onto feeling. Just flowing with the river inside. Letting it drift and float.

Now, remember your last gratitude exercise: being grateful for breath, family, friends, experience. Of all those things and people and experiences that you are grateful for, which one or two are you the most grateful for? What gives you the deepest feeling of gratitude?

Okay, now breathe softly and open your eyes.

Hold onto the thoughts of those things you are most grateful for—we will be using them in a minute.

Let's discuss another important function of the will. When we are disposed to think of ourselves in a less than flattering light, we need an instrument that gives us a boost. It is hard to let the abundance of a grateful universe flow into our lives when we feel we don't deserve it. It is hard to feel worthy of a noble purpose when we are feeling "less than."

These feelings of being "less than" or not belonging or not deserving may not be at the conscious level. They can be disguised by lots of other feelings. Some may include righteous indignation, fat or other body issues, obsessions or addictions, self-sabotage, being overly sensitive to others' opinions, needing to impress, feelings of lack, poverty consciousness, and so on. It is important to recognize even the tiniest bit of these feelings in our selves. It shows that we think we are not deserving children of God.

The will can be used to help us regain our perspective. "Deserve" statements are used to reinforce our gratitude and implement an attitude of purpose, trust, and abundance.

Now—remembering those things you felt most grateful for, compose some "deserve" statements incorporating them. (See Examples and Deserve Statement Worksheet at the end of this chapter.) Take your time; make them concise and spare. If you are uncomfortable with the phrase "a child of God," leave it out or make up your own. Notice how in each of the examples, there is an element of giving back: in the first, there is helping my friends, and in the second there is sharing.

Try to include in each of your statements an element of giving. For friends, it may be loyalty, help, compassion. For opportunity, it may be teaching, service, extra effort. For spiritual growth, it may be volunteer work, increased practice, devotion, prayer. From these elements of giving, our purpose will become apparent. If we are not certain of our purpose, doing "deserve" statements will help give us a direction.

Put together two or three statements that you feel comfortable with. For one week, write out the two or three most important parts of your gratitude 10 times each every day as "deserve" statements. The writing will burn the statements into your consciousness, accomplishing a number of things.

First, it will work on your unconscious feelings of not deserving all that life has to offer. Second, it will help develop your sense of purpose. Third, it will supply the fuel for putting unstoppable motivation behind your purpose.

Write out your deserve statements every day for a week. If you have a friend or mate whom you trust enough, say them out loud every day for a week. Tape them on a recorder and repeat them to yourself as often as you can. Inundate yourself with deserving!

Do this as often as you have to in order to move past "less than" feelings. We will be doing other things that affect self-esteem, but this is one of the most powerful.

The last important function of will is to make a commitment, "to pledge in trust or bind oneself to a certain line of conduct" as the dictionary says. The will is used to put intent into *action.*

The will is where the decision to begin, to act, takes place. Placing the will behind our purpose imbues it with unbelievable power and genius. It makes us unstoppable and overwhelming. Enthusiasm becomes a way of breathing. It is so incredible as to be discounted by most people as oversimplified and childish. Yet, the simple joy and enthusiasm of a child is Godlike and totally infectious. It cannot be denied!

Put the power of the will behind your gratitude and feel the world expand and open for you. The gift of will makes it all possible. We were all given will. Very few use it fully and in line with gratitude. Some use it partially, and have some limited areas of abundance.

To gain it all, put the will in line with gratitude. The results will be more than you can imagine, and you will begin to know that which is beyond material wealth and abundance. You will touch the spiritual well of plenty. The value of life will be apparent.

It takes work and practice to develop the will and use it in line with balanced pursuits. We have wants and needs that are not always a true measure of where we are. Usually we limit what the universe is prepared to give us by thinking too small and too narrowly.

We think, "If I just had enough money, everything else would be fine." Or, "If I could just work out this relationship with my wife (ex-wife, boyfriend, boss, mother, etc.), everything would be perfect." Or, "When I'm through with school, and have paid off my debt, then everything will fall into place."

We have a tendency to look at one thing and to think that making that thing okay will make life okay. We tend to look outside, thinking it will fix how we feel inside. By working on one area of life, the rest of our life will be fine. It hardly ever happens that way. New problems crop up, new situations in the relationship, new problems at work, new bills for the doctor, new wants, new needs.

If we are to be satisfied and fulfilled, we need a different approach. By acknowledging that everything we need and want is already in our lives through gratitude, we start the process. By putting the power of will behind our purpose, we get all that we deserve.

By understanding that it is already here in this moment, I can relax into the bounty of the universe, and know that my will is moving me even further into completion, moment by moment.

To have more, I need to be more. To be more, I will to become more. By becoming more, I have more to give, which allows me to receive more. Can you see the cycle?

The universe operates on "deserve," not need. To deserve more (and I already have plenty, but I will to *give* more), I must become more. That requires an act of will (deciding and taking action). Becoming more allows me to give more, as I have more to give! Because I am giving more, the universe gives me more. It never fails! Give more and you receive more—always!

It is truly incredible how simple it is. Our Higher Power, in Its majesty, does not play favorites. If you give more, you get more, perhaps not always the *way* you wanted or anticipated, nor always *when* you wanted it, but you always *get* it.

Every religious and spiritual tradition has a law of compensation: "You will reap what you have sown," "What goes around, comes around," the Law of Karma, and many others. Yet we never really take a close look at that. It is a "can't miss" reality.

Here's how we take advantage of that reality. We become full of gratitude for our lives and the lessons and opportunities available to us. We determine a sense of purpose for using this wonderful gift we have been given. We let go the concerns and irritations of the past. We put the power of the will behind our purpose. Soon, we are giving through our sense of purpose an unbelievable bounty to the universe, and it is pouring a bounty back to us.

If we still are frustrated and unfulfilled, we look very closely at the issue of "deserve." Perhaps we are harboring a secret thought of inferiority. Maybe we are feeling "less than," or some other subtle or not so subtle self-defeating or self-sabotaging attitude. If so, we do the "deserve" statement exercise to move in line with our will.

We remember that we are all unlimited children of God, given equal opportunity to use our will and to give back to others. We are all given equal opportunity to partake of the wonders of the universe. Maybe we all don't have equal talent or intellect in all areas, but we all have equal opportunity to give of what we *do* have, and to develop to our maximum potential our ability to give.

Now is the time to make it happen. If our lives are to have meaning, then let it start now! Put the power of the will behind your purpose and turn your focus into a laser beam, no distractions, no reservations, no conditions. Let it loose!

Here is an exercise that will help you turn your will into the lens that focuses your purpose and desire. It requires discipline and a burning desire to *be* more, to *have* more, to *give* more. It must be an overwhelming passion to grow, to reach God, and to help others. You must want more from life!

It starts with developing a few simple "will" statements. Will statements are very similar to "deserve" statements. (In fact, they can be derived directly from those statements.) It takes the openness and equality of deserving and places the power of choice behind it through the will.

Develop two or three (more is too much). These "will" statements will narrow down the scope of our attention for the next six months or so. They are incorporated in our long-term goals and purpose, but they are targeted at what is necessary for the next few months.

Let's start with a few of the examples we've already used from our gratitude and deserve work. One of the things I'm most grateful for is the friends active in my life. Part of my purpose is to develop and nurture friendships as I have a lot to give and I deserve to have great friends.

Another thing I am grateful for is the opportunities to grow spiritually and to teach the lessons I've learned. This is also a big part of my sense of purpose.

I want to continue growing and expanding, to have more and to give more. So, I develop my "will" statements for the next six months. (See Examples and Will Statement Worksheet at the end of this chapter.)

Let's take a look at a few of the elements of these "will" statements. First, they are specific as to actions and time.

Next, they all include the word "comfortably." No one says lessons need to be learned the hard way. Why not invite the universe to provide for us comfortably? There is no need to make growth harder than it is. Ask the will to provide the easiest way, and see how it strives to make that happen.

I include the phrase " a child of God." Some people use "a deserving child of God." One workshop participant used "an unlimited child of God." This is just to remind the will and the ego that we accept the bounty of the universe. We are deserving children of God, who can delight and play in the kingdom, in all its glory and plenty!

By putting the power of the will behind my intent, I aid myself and the universe in reaching my potential. I also include a phrase about "if they are open" for my friends. It is to remind me of humility and seeing the needs of others as *they* see them, not as I see them.

Lastly, I include a "will" statement of what I am willing to do in return for the wonderful gifts and growth I will and have received. The willingness to give in return opens the door even further for the bounty of the universe to pour through.

Remember the universal truth of receiving what one deserves, not what one needs. The reaping will be a result of the sowing. Of course, the bounty of the universe is so great that the returns are always greater than what's been sown. That is not the reason to give, however. Expecting a greater return than what is given is not a "big" purpose. Remember to think about your potential for giving. How do you measure up to that?

To put the power and focus of will into play, start tonight by writing out your "will" statements. Keep them brief and to the point. Make no more than two or three for the major areas of your life: maybe one for spiritual and one for relationships, or one for physical and one for financial, or one for any special area of growth.

When you have written out your statements, put them in the format of: **"I, _____, a child of God, will to comfortably _____."** Don't worry if you're not totally satisfied with the way they read. You will be changing them somewhat as you do the exercise over the next three weeks. Then, every night for the next three weeks, write out each "will" statement 10 times like you did the "deserve" statements. Do this for each of your "will" statements, followed by your statement of gift or service in return.

I promise you, by the end of those three weeks, your sense of purpose will be razor sharp. You will be totally focused. Of course it takes work. Of course not everybody is willing to sacrifice the hour of television or reading required to do this each night. Not too many people are leading a life of plenty and fulfillment, either, and very few are spiritually rich and generous!

Review your "will" statements every morning when you wake up, and if you meditate or visualize, use them in your practice. Record them on a cassette and listen to them often. Burn them into your consciousness!

It is very simple, but not always easy, although you may be surprised at the reward of just sticking to a daily discipline. For many, the reward is in the doing, but there is even greater reward later.

There are many who say, "It is not the destination, but the journey." Theirs is the philosophy of stopping to smell the roses and enjoying life day by day. I am not one to deny that. What I will add, though, is this: having a purpose (a meaningful destination) makes the journey much more valuable. *Where* you travel is as important as *how* you travel, and vice versa.

My intent colors every thing I do in life. If my will is used to move me towards a mighty purpose, a noble endeavor, then richness and flavor is added to everything I do, see, feel, touch, and savor. The meaning of life becomes part of every moment for me—no lingering in the past or straining for the future. *This* moment is rich! *This* instant holds it all! It is that "bliss" that Joseph Campbell speaks of so eloquently.

If I do my "will" statement exercises and use that practice to increase my gratitude, then the richness of existence increases magically. So much more is available. It is a spellbinding experience of the vastness of the bounty in the universe, a gift from God to us all.

We'll go further into the will as we discuss forgiveness of self and others. By this time it should be apparent to you something very special is available through these exercises. Even if you only do this partway and half-heartedly, not believing any of it, you will be receiving benefits by now.

We will move on to irritations, part two, then forgiveness, then into a few other areas that will enhance your path. Forgiveness is the last key for removing blocks to gratitude and plenty. When we are done with the forgiveness process, the ability to grow and manifest at will is yours, *with no limitations*. You may find that an outrageous statement. It is true. The only limits you have are in your thinking.

To sum up: Start with "deserve" statements for one week. In the second week, do both "deserve" and "will" statements. For the last two weeks, do only "will" statements. This gives you one month of intense, focused work. If you stick with it, you will be amazed how it works out.

Take a minute now to become grateful. Feel the flow of an expanding and plentiful universe around you, full of love, grace, harmony, and peace. Know that you are moving directly into the embrace of God and becoming one with the creator and the creation. Feel the power and passion of life in your heart and know you are a deserving child of God!

Deserve Statement Worksheet

EXAMPLES:

I may feel most grateful for the wonderful friends in my life, who are always there and give me what I need, even when I am not aware of my needs. My "deserve" statement would be: *I, Todd Weber, a child of God, deserve great friends in my life to help and be helped by me.*

Or I may feel most grateful for the wonderful opportunities provided for me to teach and learn as I move and grow spiritually. My "deserve" statement would be: *I, Todd Weber, a child of God, deserve great opportunities to learn and grow spiritually and to share those lessons with others.*

I, _____, a child of God, deserve:

S/He, _____, a child of God, deserves:

You, _____, a child of God, deserve:

I, _____, a child of God, deserve:

S/He, _____, a child of God,
deserves:

You, _____, a child of God,
deserve:

I, _____, a child of God,
deserve:

S/He, _____, a child of God,
deserves:

You, _____, a child of God,
deserve:

I, _____, a child of God,
deserve:

📝 Will Statement Worksheet

EXAMPLES:

I, Todd Weber, a child of God, will to comfortably be spiritually active and growing—teaching my Workshop gratitude and forgiveness for the next six months.

*I, Todd Weber, a child of God, will to comfortably nurture and protect my friends by sharing my spiritual growth, **if they are open**, for the next six months.*

In return, I, Todd Weber, a child of God, will to comfortably give service, discipline, compassion and love in abundance to all and beyond expectation of return.

I, _____, a child of God, will to comfortably:

S/He, _____, a child of God, wills to comfortably:

You, _____, a child of God, will to comfortably:

I, _____, a child of God, will to comfortably:

S/He, _____, a child of God, wills to comfortably:

You, _____, a child of God, will to comfortably:

I, _____, a child of God, will to comfortably:

S/He, _____, a child of God, wills to comfortably:

You, _____, a child of God, will to comfortably:

I, _____, a child of God, will to comfortably:

In return, I, _____, a child of God, will to comfortably give:

✍ Mirror Exercise

The last exercise for the will involves taking a look at the whole package, so far. Review your gratitude exercises, take a look at your "deserve" and "will" statements. Then, stand or sit facing a mirror where you can look at your face and eyes closely.

Looking into your own eyes, review your gratitude list, then repeat your "will " statements. If there is any hesitancy in making strong, emotional "will" statements, or if you have to look away, then renew your gratitude and deserve exercises. You must be able to look directly into your eyes and see the purpose and resolve focused there.

Practice this exercise until you are comfortable looking deeply and directly at yourself while practicing gratitude and "will."

Irritations Revisited

It is liberating to release and let go of these hooks.
—*Workshop participant*

Let's review irritations, frustration, anger, impatience, and little hurts again. When we first did the irritation list exercise, we did it from the perspective of the damage and hurt others had done to us, and we released that damage or hurt and the necessity to buffer or hide from it in our body and spirit. This is a powerful and wonderful exercise. Many people report startling body and emotional changes, feelings of peace, and weight lifted from them through the practice of this exercise.

The perspective this time will be on issues dealing with us: not what others have done to us, but *our* reactions, fears, withholding, etc. to what is going on. We will "get current." This is more in line with a Tenth Step inventory. In addition to amends, we need to release the negative feelings we hold against ourselves.

We are going to use the exercise again in order to let go of the smaller disappointments, hurts, bad habits, resentments, guilts, and other negative feelings that we hold against *ourselves*. This is not for major acts or incidences for which we feel guilt. We will be doing a self-forgiveness process for that. This is for releasing the petty, small, distracting, little things we dislike about ourselves.

IRRITATION LIST EXAMPLES:

Feeling guilty about ignoring my family	I can let go of that
Feeling bad about being impatient for more growth	I can let go of that
Being judgmental and negative	I can let go of that
Wanting my partner to change	I can let go of that
Getting defensive with my friend	I can let go of that
Being rigid about belief	I can let go of that
Being afraid to start the new project	I can let go of that
Having doubts about my current course	I can let go of that
Not being able to be grateful *all* the time	I can let go of that

and so on.

As you can see, the list is made up of current, and some not-so-current, things that are not exactly the way I want them in my life. They have to do with character traits, resentments, feelings, habits, or lacks that I see as "bad."

First, this is not to judge myself or put myself down. This practice is for naming things and letting them go. It is about feelings. Feelings are not right or wrong, good or bad, they just *are*! But I am my own worst critic, and I imagine that you might be pretty hard on yourself, too.

So in looking at how I feel now about myself, and being grateful for the wonderful opportunities I have to change and grow, I can name those traits, feelings, habits, etc. that I'd like to change, and release them. This exercise lets me take the "charge" out of those damaging feelings about myself. It lets me create distance between myself and my actions. It gives me some detachment.

This allows me to be totally committed to the purpose of my actions, and released from the results. I can detach from "wanting" or "needing" a certain outcome if I am totally behind the purpose and will of the action in the now. The results take care of themselves, if I take care of the now! Being attached to results is one of the hardest habits to let go. We have been trained to identify with our results. Many of our parents made us think that our value as a human being is based on results—not *who we are*, but *what we do* and *how we do it*. It is an insidious and damaging view of self. Detachment is a method of gaining perspective about results. Gratitude can help provide detachment. (There is a lengthy discussion about results and detachment in *The Next Step*. If you have difficulty with this concept, try reading that section.)

Gratitude and release allow me to remain totally present. This exercise removes the "hooks" holding me to certain feelings or expectations about myself. Try this exercise for two weeks or a month every morning, or you can make it part of your Tenth Step inventory every night. (I highly recommend a written Tenth Step every night.) Write out your resentments, irritations, bad habits, hurts, and so on—and let them go. You will be impressed with what happens.

One other very important concern is addressed by this exercise. So far, we have not discussed fear in this practice. The main reason is that it is indirectly dealt with through all the exercises, but this exercise deals with fear in particular. (Again, see *The Next Step* for a more detailed discussion on fear.)

Fear may be very apparent by physical symptoms—shallow, rapid breathing, sweating, shakes, tightness of the throat, and so on—or it may be very subtle and unconscious. Fear shows up in many of the feelings and habits we've discussed. Low self-esteem is the breeding ground for fear.

It shows itself as procrastination, lateness, rigidity, defensiveness, poverty-consciousness, feelings of lack, anxiety, depression, greed, aggression, guilt, timidity—the list is endless. We have all experienced these feelings, a little or a lot. Most of the time we feel we have no control over them, and up until now, that may have been true. Now, however, we have a way of addressing these uncomfortable feelings and habits directly. First, let's take a look at the easiest approach.

Be grateful for the feeling or habit. Look at all it has taught you. Look at all the pain it has caused and what you've learned from that. Look at the awareness it brought with it as a gift.

When I was younger, there were times I was so depressed I had no idea what to do. I couldn't get out of bed. I couldn't think. I couldn't see where I was. I didn't know exactly how I was feeling. I just knew it was bad! Have you ever felt like that?

How could I ever find the gift in that experience? Well, I survived it! Nietsche said that a thing that doesn't destroy me makes me stronger, and that is what happened. I survived. I came out of the experience stronger than I went in. That is one gift—I know I can survive depression.

If that were all, it would be plenty, but there is more. I found out a lot about myself from those experiences. I found out I am a deep thinker, sometimes so deep that I can't find the thoughts myself. I found out that I feel strongly and compassionately. I am so sensitive that I had to buffer myself through withdrawal to survive and process the feelings.

I feel compassion for all who suffer similarly, as I can identify with the pain and the lessons. So, you see, it is possible to find the gifts and have gratitude for all experience. By developing gratitude, the fear is removed from the experience. I find the strength in myself, and release the negative.

If the negative or "bad" feeling or habit or resentment is active in our lives right now, then we can address it with the irritation list. Perhaps we are so involved in "being" the problem that we can't see the good in it to be grateful. If we can name it, or part of it, and start releasing and letting go of it, we gain some detachment.

By continuing this exercise, more detachment is gained and the power of the habit or feeling is diffused, so we can begin to look for the good. What have we gained from the experience? Maybe it is only being able to name it. That puts us way ahead of where we were. If we can name it, we can ask for help, and gain detachment day by day in order to let it go.

Here is a chance to put your foot on the accelerator! If you want to grow, to change, to take charge of your life, to be more, here it is. Practice the exercises you've been given, then really hit the irritation list on self. Do it!

If you do, the growth and change will be so dramatic as to astound you. You can't help but change through this process.

☞ Irritation List Worksheet

1.   I can let go of that

2.   I can let go of that

3.   I can let go of that

4.   I can let go of that

5.   I can let go of that

6.   I can let go of that

7.   I can let go of that

8.   I can let go of that

9.   I can let go of that

10.   I can let go of that

Forgiveness

> *To forgive is to cancel demands, condi-*
> *tions, and expectations which prevent*
> *the mind from maintaining the Atti-*
> *tude of Love.*
> *—from the Essene Code of Conduct*

Unconditional Love and Forgiveness, by Edith R. Stauffer, Ph.D., is the best source for working on forgiveness issues that I know. There are workshops available through Edith, myself, and other members of Psychosynthesis International, given by certified instructors, that are terrific in guiding a person through this process.

The basic meaning of "forgive," as we will be using it, is to cancel. What, then, is cancelled? What are cancelled are those things in your mind which prevent love and gratitude for self and others. Removing those things that block the love and gratitude is a mental and spiritual act. It takes place in the mind of the person doing the forgiving.

Forgiveness does not depend on external circumstances. It is not conditioned on someone else or yourself changing or asking for forgiveness or doing anything. The expectation, demand, or condition is cancelled in your own mind.

Forgiving, then, requires an acknowledgment of our own error in withdrawing or withholding our love and gratitude. We must be willing to correct that error. Forgiveness is not done for the sake of the person being forgiven. It is done in order to restore harmony and balance within ourselves. This is a key point. I repeat, *we forgive in order to restore balance and harmony within ourselves*.

This may seem like a narcissistic spiritual approach, yet the effects are powerful. If I am not in control of circumstance, chance, or results, then it is my effort and attitude that set the tone of my life. Forgiving is a method of setting straight *my* attitude. It cancels restrictions in my feelings and thoughts.

Cancelling is not pardoning. It does not wipe out the wrong of another. We cannot cancel another's action or error. It is not forgetting or clearing our memory of the wrong. *Cancelling is the dropping or removing of the requirement that the other person perform in any certain way in order to be loved.*

Forgiveness is an act which is a natural process for those who have an attitude of unconditional love and total gratitude. You cannot have unconditional love and be unforgiving. You cannot be totally grateful and be unforgiving.

Forgiving is being willing to let go of those feelings which are consuming us: anger, hurt, resentment, fear, and all the others which cause us to block our love and gratitude, insulate ourselves from the world, encapsulate our fear and anger in disease, build walls with our distrust, and limit ourselves in the name of safety.

To forgive is to be willing to get back into the flow of life and gratitude, to allow the flow of love from God to wash through us and out to the person to be forgiven. You cannot be healthy physically, mentally,

emotionally, or spiritually if you hate yourself or another. To be willing to give up that hate is to move
toward health. To unblock the hate, anger, hurt,
through forgiveness is to open the flow of love and
gratitude which nurtures and heals us.

We have cleaned up a lot of our forgiveness issues
with the irritations lists. Now it is time to clean up the
large issues that are left. The act of forgiveness lets us
finish removing the last blocks to total and complete
gratitude. If we can reach the state of complete
gratitude, moment to moment, we will have total
awareness. Nothing will be hidden from us. The total
glory of the universe will be ours.

That ought to help us be, or become, willing to
forgive. Here is the place we address Dad: all the
wrongs done us, all the unfair expectations, all the
judgments made from a damaging perspective. Here is
where we address Mom: all the nurturing not given, all
the conditional demands, all the guilt bestowed for
unclear reasons. Here is where we address wives and
ex-wives. Here is where we can work out any of the
issues left that did not get handled on the irritation list.

Start a list of those people you need to forgive.
What demand, expectation, or condition of yours was
not met which caused the incident that needs to be
forgiven? If you forgive this person, what negative
things will you give up? Do not put yourself on this list.
We will be doing a separate exercise for self-forgiveness.

Please do your list now of those people you want to
forgive. (See Forgiveness Log at the end of this chapter.) Anybody you are still harboring negative feelings
and resentments about can be on your list. Do your list,

give the expectations, demands, or conditions, and then name what you would lose if you were to forgive that person.

Forgiveness is a willingness to hold a certain attitude, to move forward, to be more comfortable and suffer less. It is the willingness to take responsibility for oneself and to allow others to take responsibility for themselves. Forgiveness is a decision *not to punish ourselves for the wrongs of others or circumstances*. It is a decision to re-enter the flow of love and life.

In doing the forgiveness process (see Forgiveness Exercise at the end of this chapter), there needs to be a conscious shift from the wrong done and your feelings about it, to the mental level of how you would have preferred it had happened. You then can say what you would have preferred. It should be very specific for each incident.

At this point, by naming what you would have preferred, you are moving toward the positive and away from the negative actions of what happened. You have changed your focus. This is why it is *very* important to state the preferences in positive terms.

When you have unconditional love and total gratitude, a part of you can see the good in others and situations. This, and the preference, allow a shift in consciousness and a loosening of the conflict or impasse. The conflict is between what you perceive (the way you saw it happen) and what you would have preferred. This conflict blocks the flow of love, which is your ability to see the good in others.

These personal demands or expectations which are blocking your flow of love and gratitude are in your mind, and you have the power to cancel them. By elevating your consciousness to your Higher Self, and having an attitude of unconditional love, you can cancel your expectations, demands, and conditions. When this happens, the flow of love and gratitude returns at an ever-increasing rate, sweeping you along in the flow of love and plenty.

 **Forgiveness Log**

EXAMPLE:

Person	Condition, Demand, Expectation	I will give up:
Mom	Didn't meet my expectation of unconditional love, nurturing, trust, and support.	Anger, fear of women, distrust, feelings of lack, feelings of unworthiness, resentment, conditions in relationships, fear of abandonment, frustration with hypocricy

I look at this example and ask myself, how much longer do I want to keep holding on to those negative feelings? How much longer do I want to keep blocking my ability to heal these wounds and get on with a healthy, glorious life? The answer is obvious. I don't want to hang on to them any longer than I have to. I am willing to move on. I want these feelings out of my life now! I am ready to forgive Mom.

Person	Condition, Demand, Expectation	I will give up:

Person	Condition, Demand, Expectation	I will give up:

 **Forgiveness Exercise***

Step 1: Say to yourself: "I choose to stop punishing myself and feeling bad for what (name of person) has done or is doing. I feel so (angry, hurt, disappointed, etc.) when you (ignore me, hit me, say so and so, etc.)."
Be specific for each incident to be forgiven.

Person   Incident

STEP 2: Imagine that the person you need to forgive is in front of you. You may wish to close your eyes. As you hold the image of this person in front of you, say aloud: "I would have preferred you had said (or done) _____." Always state the preference in positive terms: "I would have preferred that you treated me kindly," not "I would have preferred that you not treat me badly."

STEP 3: Say: "But you didn't do that, so I now will to release this incident. I choose to let it go and be free of it."

STEP 4: Say: "Therefore, I cancel all demands, expectations, and conditions that you do (or say, or be for each incident) _____ in the past and now. I cancel the demand that you be (any certain way). You are totally responsible for your actions and deeds, and I release you to your own good."

STEP 5: Close your eyes and raise your consciousness into the Higher Self. Imagine the love that the Higher Self has for you. Feel the compassion and love from the Higher Self; allow it to flow into you and release all the conditions and expectations and demands. Really feel the positive qualities of the Higher Self, that part of you that has protected, loved, and nurtured you all the days of your life.

STEP 6: With your eyes closed, continue to feel the love from the Higher Self and now say to the person you are forgiving: "I send this love from my Higher Self out to you just as you are and have been." Feel this love flowing out from you to this person. Take your time to feel and experience this.

STEP 7: Now be aware of your body and how it feels. See if you are holding on to any demands that this person change in any way. If you do not feel release, repeat the process. Repeat the process for each action you are holding against the person. The mind cannot do a blanket forgiveness—each incident must be treated separately. Always examine your willingness to be free. If you do not find release, there may be another related incident that is not yet in your conscious mind. Ask: "Is something else blocking this process?" If so, it will usually come up immediately. Process what comes. If nothing comes, feel deep gratitude that you can feel love from your Higher Self and send it out to the forgiven one. The sense of relief will come.

This exercise can be done often. It works for small hurts and disappointments and it works for deep emotional trauma. It works anytime we feel love is blocked.

Unconditional Love and Forgiveness, by Edith Stauffer, ch. 15, pps. 139-140).

Forgiving Yourself

*"Some pray over things they have done
and these seem like double.
Some straightway forgive themselves
and save the Lord the trouble."*

     —Anonymous

Often, when people do things that upset them or which they view as wrong or "bad," they think that is what **they are**: "bad." They identify with their action rather than with their being.

Psychosynthesis and many other viewpoints make a distinct separation between you and your actions. You have responsibility for the unkind act, but you are also capable of kind, thoughtful actions for which you are also responsible.

You need to look clearly at yourself, without faults in your mind. Most people are much kinder and more forgiving to a stranger than they are to themselves. When this is true, it is an indication that there is work to do on self-esteem. We need to see ourselves as we see others—clearly, and with compassion, openness, and acceptance.

We need to become aware of the fact that we can change our actions at *will*. We can be in charge of ourselves. We need to appreciate the fact that we are connected to our Higher Self. Through gratitude, no matter what, we can regain the awareness of our connection. Through our Higher Self we are connected to God. This understanding gives us a view of who we really are.

In the Aramaic and Greek languages, the word "sin" is an archery term which means *"missing the mark— not achieving the goal expected."* According to those who spoke the Aramaic language, if you miss the mark, the next step is to determine why, make the needed adjustments, take another step, draw your bow, and aim again. Then let it fly!

In Western culture, missing the mark is considered a great and terrible action. Sin in some Western minds is irreparable. People act as if they are ruined for life. They think they are bad and that there is no good in them. The guilt requires punishment, or so they reason. The punishment may be in the form of:

Depriving ourselves of adventures and opportunities;

Depriving ourselves of rewarding and enjoyable relationships;

Depressing ourselves into "black" funks;

Telling ourselves we have no right to live and wishing to die;

Developing physical or emotional "dis-ease" and illness.

Sometimes people repress the memory of missing the mark without dealing with it. It may not be the way they want to handle the problem, but they do not have a means of forgiveness to handle it correctly. Repression is the one way they know to survive.

When you suppress or repress incidents that have bothered you, the same activity continues in the lower unconsciousness. The same punishment goes on from a different place—your unconscious mind. With the unconscious, you project your "punisher" into the environment. It is "they" who hold you back from what you deserve. It is "circumstance" that got in the way of success. It can remain in your unconscious for a long time, and result in many diseases and illnesses.

You can become conscious of your mistakes, identify with them long enough to learn the lesson they have to offer, and then *let them go!* You then allow the healing, soothing love of the Higher Self to flow through you. The Higher Self can direct the healing energy of God where it is needed and allow you to open to unconditional love and gratitude.

After you have been successful in your own forgiveness, you may find the opportunity to help others in forgiving themselves. Most people carry a heavy burden of guilt because they have not learned to forgive themselves. It will be a real act of humility and service to be able to be on their level of awareness and lovingly help them in this way.

Self-forgiveness Exercise

1. Sit quietly in a chair in an attitude of seeking, openness, and repentance (sorrow for what happened). Raise your consciousness to your Higher Self. Ask your Higher Self to forgive you for _____ (naming one incident at a time). Know and believe that your Higher Self is eager to restore the flow of love to your consciousness again.

Rest a moment after making contact with your Higher Self.

2.   Stand so you can look down on the place where you were seated. With your eyes closed, imagine (as the Higher Self) looking down on your personal self. Assume the attitudes of the Higher Self. Remember the qualities of love, compassion, understanding and wisdom. If you are feeling sorrow, guilt, or unease, you are still identified with the personal self.

From this elevated place, with wisdom and understanding, you can see all the circumstances of the past. You can see why and how everything happened as it did.

Identifying with the great compassion of the Higher Self, send your Unconditional Love in abundance to the personal self, and cancel all conditions the personal self is holding. Assure the personal self that no expectation, demand, or condition can separate your love from it.

3.   Assume the position of the personal self sitting in the chair again.   Take time to identify with the personal self that has been forgiven. Feel how it is to be forgiven—the slate wiped clean. Feel your freedom. Feel the healing forgiveness fill you. With deep gratitude in your heart, thank the Higher Self for the forgiveness you have experienced.

It is important to get the perspective of height when doing step 2 as the Higher Self. If possible, do the exercise on a set of stairs, with the personal self on the bottom and the Higher Self at the top. It will help in the exercise.

The Will Revisited

It shifted my perspective of circumstances in my life from that of being a victim in opposition to my conditions to being filled with wonder at the wisdom, the lessons, the gift of happenings.
—Workshop participant

Forgiveness exercises are tremendous, but it is like peeling an onion. Layer after layer must be addressed in order to completely release the emotional, physical, and spiritual "hooks" that hang us up. Great weight is lifted from us in releasing all this emotional residue. A few people may have difficulty with being open enough to forgive themselves or others. For whatever reason, their capacity for forgiveness, growth, gratitude, love, happiness, etc. has been limited. Maybe they have been so beaten down from life and experience they have no hope or belief left. Maybe they have become so cynical there is no room for anything else. Maybe it is just too much effort to make a change.

Does any of this apply to you? Even just a little? Are you growing, giving, and becoming as much as you had hoped? Are you still hung up on forgiveness issues? Still finding it difficult to be grateful? Would you like to enhance your ability to change, to become more, be more, have more, and give more, no matter where you are starting from?

We are going to look again at the greatest gift God gave to us: the will. This time we are going to look at it in a different context, and find out exactly how powerful it really is.

A universal principle is that if your cup is full, you can't pour any more in. If you do, it just runs over the sides and is wasted. In fact, there is a wonderful Zen parable about this principle:

A seeker, who had been studying for years, came to visit a Zen master. The master greeted him, asked him inside, and gave him a comfortable place to sit. The seeker proceeded to tell the master all the things he had studied during his quest. He went on and on. The master interrupted the seeker to ask if he would like some tea. The seeker acknowledged that he would like tea, and continued with his recitation. The master started to pour a cup of tea for the seeker. The cup filled quickly and the master kept pouring. The cup overflowed onto the tray, and the master kept pouring. Finally, the seeker noticed what was happening and said, "Stop! What are you doing?" The master replied, "You are like this cup. You are so full of yourself that there is no room for new knowledge."

So in order to grow, receive more, learn more, become more grateful, we must empty our cups, even if it is only just a little bit. We must use the will to direct ourselves to empty some out. If we are full of conceit, anger, distrust, or misery, we must get rid of some in order to receive what we want. If we are full of pride, knowledge, expertise, or contentment, we must empty some out. We have to use the will to do this.

Here is how it works: If I want more gratitude in my life, I must give away gratitude. I must teach it , show it , practice it, even if only a little. This is the only way to create more space. I must share what I have in order to receive more!

The amazing thing is that the universe expands the container to a larger capacity when the contents are shared. If I share a little of my gratitude, I get much more back, and I get the ability to be more grateful. As I give more away, the vessel gets larger.

It never fails. If I share what I have, I get more in return and I am able to share more, which in turn gives me more, so I have more to give, and it continues. But I must make it happen. *I must act!* It requires an act of will to take the first step, and to keep going. I must be committed.

Lets take a look at a few examples from my own experience of how this works:

I wanted to grow spiritually, become more, and move toward God. I have been given an insight that gratitude is one of the most direct paths for making this happen. So, using the will, I decided to become more grateful. I practiced gratitude exercises. I shared this experience with others. My gratitude grew. I had further insights. I practiced irritation lists. I shared these with others. I talked about the results. I got excited. My gratitude grew. I started a Workshop with which to practice gratitude. I shared my experiences and insights. I got more insights and experiences. My gratitude grew. I decided to write a book. I started sharing the ideas and exercises with the group and other people. I saw changes happening in their lives due to gratitude. My gratitude grew.

I wanted more money in my life. I was tired of being in debt and scrambling to keep up. I had always been able to generate income; it was controlling spending where I had problems. I knew there were two ways to help myself out: make more money and cut back on expenses.

In order to make more money, I had to be worth more. To be worth more, I had to become more. I wasn't sure how this would happen. I just knew that it would be hard to work more hours, so to increase my income I had to make myself worth more for each hour worked. I needed to become more valuable.

I made a will statement about increasing my value by a certain date, and set out to become more. I became involved in a growth and success group. I worked on myself to be more aware of giving service, to give more than was expected in return for my pay, and to give more than I had previously.

In order to give more, I worked with the growth group to have more substance to my being and aware-ness, more power, more focus.

The more I was able to give in service, the more I was able to grow with the group. Then, out of nowhere (I thought), came a job offer for the amount of money I had set as my goal. I had targeted reaching it in three years. It happened in four months!

At the same time, I developed a monthly spending plan. I never before had budgeted or stuck to a plan. This time, I made a plan based on the book *The Richest Man In Babylon*, by George Clason. I made sure that the first check I wrote every month gave 10% of my net income after taxes to charity, usually the food bank. Then I saved 10%, invested 10% in my education or career, and lived off the rest.

In an amazingly short period of time, I had more money in the bank, more money to give away, and more money to spend than I ever imagined. I took it one step at a time and gave first. I didn't wait until I had the income to start giving 10% away and saving 10%. I did it when I couldn't even make ends meet. I gave it away when it hurt. Second, I saved it.

Immediately, things started happening in my life to provide for me, maybe not exactly the way I had envisioned it, or exactly in the time frame I had hoped, but it happened, some of it much faster than I ever could have imagined.

My story is not unique. Many people have reported exactly the same kind of turnaround. It accelerates when the element of total gratitude is added. Being grateful gives new meaning to what I already have, makes me thankful for the new things in my life, and gives me new vision to see opportunity that I never knew existed.

Those examples are just minor changes that are available for those who are *willing to take action*! It must be a willing decision. I don't want to live this way any more. I want to be more, have more, give more, become more. I am going to act!

When that decision is made, all sorts of things happen to help us out. Like the quote from Goethe, "Boldness has genius, power and magic in it!" God made us all big. Giving makes us aware of it.

Take action! Do the exercises. Invest fifteen minutes to half an hour a day in becoming more, in having more to give, in being a person of gratitude.

Will Statement Worksheet

Develop a will statement to practice for three weeks, dealing with one of the following areas: giving, teaching, or sharing. Put this into *action* in your life.

EXAMPLES:

I, [your name], an unlimited child of God, will to comfortably *give* ...; **or**

I, [your name], an unlimited child of God, will to comfortably *teach* ...; **or**

I, [your name], an unlimited child of God, will to comfortably *share* ....

Just as with the previous will statements, write this statement out ten times each day for three weeks. Record it and play it often. Say it to a friend or mate. Make it part of your life.

I, _____, an unlimited child of God, will to comfortably:

S/He, _____, an unlimited child of God, wills to comfortably:

You, _____, an unlimited child of God, will to comfortably:

I, _____, an unlimited child of God, will to comfortably:

S/He, _____, an unlimited child of God, wills to comfortably:

You, _____, an unlimited child of God, will to comfortably:

I, _____, an unlimited child of God, will to comfortably:

S/He, _____, an unlimited child of God, wills to comfortably:

You, _____, an unlimited child of God, will to comfortably:

In return, I, _____, an unlimited child of God, will to comfortably give:

Meditation

*He who knows that enough is enough
will always have enough.*

—*Lao Tze*

Meditation is a method of quieting the mind (the ego) and gaining access to that stillness and wisdom inside. In the West, it is "Be still and know that I am God." In the East, it is different forms of making contact with the "Self" or God by quieting the mind through breath awareness or Mantra or other practices.

There are also methods of chanting and single-pointed awareness and breathing, all meant as a path to stillness and awareness. The masters are said to be in that state at all times, where every breath and action is a meditation and they are connected with God and the mysteries of the universe.

There are many good books on meditation and the many different philosophies and practices of obtaining awareness and realization, both East and West. Ram Dass is a good source. Tarthang Tulku has excellent books on the Tibetan Buddhist approach to meditation. Steven Levine's book, *A Gradual Awakening*, is excellent. I read a ton of them looking for "the answer."

I also tried to hear or see every "master" or teacher I could find, hoping to find the path to God. I planned to go to India and other countries with a long spiritual history and culture in hopes of finding a guru or teacher who would help me on the path. I desperately wanted to experience higher consciousness and move into spiritual growth with peace and serenity and wholeness as a reward.

I tried vegetarianism and fasting. I tried silence and retreat. I searched everywhere, except at the heart of my own gratitude.

One day it came to me that what I sought was already here. It always was and always would be. I was not aware of it because I was too busy looking, judging, analyzing, negating, and seeing the lack in my life, instead of the good. I became aware of a quiet flow of insight and wisdom, grace, peace, and wonder, that at some level had always been there. I remembered feeling that sense of wonder and joy and freedom when I was a child. I felt connected to it all.

It takes the will. With gratitude, all is available. Everything! No limits. Let's take a few minutes to experience directly what I mean.

Meditation Exercise

Find a comfortable place to sit. Sit quietly, relax, and allow your breathing to soften and slow down. Let the mind flow where it will. Don't give it any hooks or Velcro for the thoughts to catch on. Just let it flow.

Now, remember all the things you are grateful for, all the things that have meaning in your life, and thank God and the universe for those blessings.

Thank God and the universe for family. For all the love and support and giving and acceptance of family. For all the experiences of pain and distrust and conflict and argument that strengthened you and gave you growth. For all the experiences and lessons of togetherness and sharing. For all those gifts that made you who you are and gave you the ability to become more.

Thank God and the universe for friends. For loyalty and sharing and confidence. For acceptance and conspiracy. For betrayal and grief. For all those experiences that let you grow and become.

Thank God and the universe for hearing. For beautiful music and loud chimes. For baby crying and wail of grief. For shouts of joy and moans of pleasure. For soaring whistle and roar of falls.

Thank God and the universe for sight. For colors bright and dull. For dazzling white and matte black. For patterns and designs and random scrawls and splatter. For the beauty of light. For sunsets and sunrises. For the intricacy of nature and shape of form.

Thank God and the universe for touch. For the feel of silk and sandpaper. For soft caress and hard wood. For the warmth of loving hug and the sting of a slap. For the hot and cold of summer and winter.

Thank God and the universe for taste. For sweet and sour and salty and bitter. For explosion of flavor and hot and spicy.

Thank God and the universe for smell. For fresh baked bread and compost heap. For sweet perfume and stale sweat. For baby's breath and old mildew.

Thank God and the universe for feelings. For joy and love and comfort. For disgust and revulsion and dismay. For the experience of ecstasy and misery. For anger and fear. For frustration and impatience. For openness and compassion. For humor and contentment. For the experience of contrast that sharpens and deepens it all.

Thank God and the Universe for the ability to think. For the soaring sweep of genius and the slow plodding of deduction. For memory and intuition. For learning and forgetting. For naming and knowing.

Thank God and the universe for choice. For giving us the will. For being able to become more, have more, give more. For being able to choose to stay the same or change. What a gift!

Thank God for it all. For the majesty and mystery and expression of it all.

Sit quietly in the gratitude and sense the tide of creation and spaciousness, love and peace, compassion and plenty, flowing through and around you. Feel your connection with the flow of the universe. Don't worry if thoughts intrude or worries interrupt. Just thank them gently for their message and return to gratitude for the blessings received. Don't expect anything. Just remain open and thankful.

Try doing this for two weeks. Every morning just after completing your gratitude list, sit quietly and go into the flow of gratitude. As your practice deepens, you will gain further and deeper knowledge, and you will "know" directly the sense of God and the universe.

Prayer

Thanks, God! What joy when I remember to be thankful!
—Workshop participant

Prayer is our song of thanks to God and the universe. We thank God for the endless bounty and grace available to us, and for the ability to be grateful and grow and become. Since everything we could need or want is already available, there is no reason to pray for fulfillment of needs or desires.

However, there are times when it is hard to pray with gratitude: in the middle of a divorce when I am full of pain, guilt, and feelings of worthlessness and failure, anger, frustration, self-pity, and worry; or when I have just lost my job, I am deeply in debt, and my car breaks down.

At times like these, prayers of thanksgiving are very hard. It is almost impossible to see the gift in the situation, or even want to try to see it. We become so caught up in the circumstances and feelings that we have no inclination or desire to thank God and be grateful. We cannot see the good at all.

This is when grace saves us. If we are open, even the tiniest little bit, to using our will to change the situation, God and the universe will help us out. If we can ask our Higher Power to help us develop the will to change, it will improve immediately.

A prayer to seek God's help in using our will to become more, have more, give more, be more will make things happen. The process of taking responsibility for our own situation and using the will to change it puts the whole power of the universe behind the change. It may not be easy. We may be so caught up in negative feelings and so totally identified with the problem that we don't use the will to move us toward God, Who gives us the perspective and vision to see solutions and the lesson being offered.

There is *always* a gift or lesson in any situation. It may take time and distance to see it, but it is always there. Through gratitude, we can gain detachment and perspective and see the gift in the circumstance. If we can't be grateful, then we *can* pray for God's help in developing gratitude and the will to change.

If we ask God's help to help ourselves, there is always an answer. If we just want a solution, without helping or changing ourselves, then usually not much happens. If we pray for help to use our will to become different—more, giving, grateful—there is always a response.

In Twelve Step programs, some people get confused about prayer and meditation. It can be difficult to know which prayers to use and how to pray. Since the Twelve Step programs are non-religious, they are very careful about giving instructions.

The Eleventh Step in the program is "Sought through prayer and meditation to improve our conscious contact with God *as we understood Him*, praying only for knowledge of His will for us and the power to carry that out."

God's greatest gift to us is free will: the power to make our own decisions and the ability to invoke the will and make changes. Perhaps seeking to align our will *with* God's will is more appropriate and effective.

To look only for God's will as an instrument for change is to release responsibility and accountability. God's will is manifest! He said "let there be light" and there was light. His thought is reality. To think that there is any doubt of His will is to doubt our senses and experience.

I believe that God's will for us is to be all we can be through our own efforts. He endowed us with tremendous potential and said "grow." He didn't limit it by saying how or when, He just said go for your potential. Our prayer should be to maximize *our* will through willingness, to empower our ability to change faster and more. Giving up accountability limits our self-esteem and our power to make choices. Gratitude shows us through direct experience that the magnificence of the universe is ours. God gave all of us this gift. We are deserving children of God. Saying otherwise limits our growth and potential.

Staying only within the Steps may limit those folks working a recovery program. Perhaps it is time to move on to a larger, more open, and descrving model of recovery. Some experts say we are all dysfunctional and codependent in some manner. We all have the means to move beyond it, if we accept responsibility for whcre we are and use the will to decide to move on.

Rather than decide about this on whether it is "right" or "wrong," try to keep an open mind. "Right" is an issue that is only important if we're rigid and defensive. In *The Next Step* I spend a considerable amount of time discussing emotional issues tied to being "right." I ask you not to make a judgment based on *thinking* about it.

Please try the exercises on gratitude and irritations, *then* decide if there is power available in your life to change at will. Pray in thanksgiving and gratitude. If you can't do that, then pray for help in developing the will to move into gratitude. Your life will change. Your perspective will expand. You will see more, understand more, and be able to give more, and life will give you more, in return. (For more help with prayer, see the *12 Step Prayer Book*, Glen Abbey Books, 1990.)

 # Prayer Exercise

Once again, for one week, try this exercise:

Start each day with a prayer of thanksgiving. As part of your gratitude meditation, end your meditation with a prayer of thanks. Give thanks for all that is available in your life *now*. Give a prayer of true "appreciation" for your life.

After trying that for a week, when you are ready, try a different prayer. This time for one week start each day with a prayer for willingness—to grow and change, to see things differently, to align your life with higher principles. Use your will statements as a guide, and pray to develop willingness.

After completing each week of prayer, decide whether you'd like to continue praying this way. Devise your own prayer (maybe a combination prayer) and perhaps seek humility to be able to see the needs of others "as they see them" and respond to those needs if practical.

You will see your prayer practice mature and deepen. It will complement every part of your spiritual pursuit.

Innocence

*I feel so much more alive. I feel like I'm
glowing, radiating love. I am a wide-eyed
child again!*

—*Workshop participant*

By becoming grateful, we return to a state of innocence. By gaining access directly to the flow of the
universe, we regain the joy of discovery. Everything
becomes new again and we can be thankful for it. Life
takes on a sparkle and a freshness that is captivating. We
are captured totally by the now.

When we practice gratitude, we are propelled into a
state where we naturally know the correct way to go, be,
and do for us. Because of the connection with the Higher
Self and God, through gratitude, we are in line with
universal principles. We become totally effective—direct,
simple, powerful. There is a childlike innocence and
grace to spiritually aligned people. Becoming aligned
through gratitude gives us that innocence and grace.

Do the exercises! Meditate on gratitude and your
blessings. Use your will to move toward God. In return,
you get innocence, grace, joy, and the wonder of renew-
ing your life.

Innocence is a state of trust in the process of the
universe. If we give, we will receive—always. If we give
more, we will receive and grow more—always. Put the
energy out, make a sustained, intense effort with a pur-

pose, and you will get it all. Trust the process. Return to innocence.

Innocence implies unlimited generosity. In our innocence, we can give all, trusting in the process. Being generous is its own reward. We gain fulfillment and satisfaction. We grow and expand. We delight in the play of life and its patterns. We laugh with joy for the gifts of being able to give and receive. We are totally grateful for life.

Innocence means growth. Being innocent, we are open to possibility, not rigid and calcified in our belief. We glow with the satisfaction of expansion and discovery. Making new connections, directly experiencing life and creation, and gaining new insights become natural again. It is magical.

Innocence is being in the now. With gratitude, we remain here. There is no escaping to the past or worrying over past mistakes, no flights of fancy into the future, no bringing thoughts of tomorrow's problems, catastrophes, and crises to worry over today. There are just the gifts of now, and joy in the present and all it has to offer.

Thank this day for its gifts! Thank the flow for its ever present gifts. In gratitude, we are totally here—available for the bounty of the universe. We are ready for all the experiences that make us more, all the insights that allow us to give, all the pain that permits us to appreciate health, all the sorrow that gives depth and context to joy. We can see all the incredible vistas of possibility and choice. Thank this day for being able to shape it through will.

Innocence Exercise

Today, for fun and play, I will do something nice to help someone—in secret.

Emotions

*Emotions, thoughts, flashes of insight,
even my body, seem more like they are
working together rather than being at
odds with each other.*
—Workshop participant

Emotions are the language of the soul. Emotions *move* us to be and grow. They also move us to withdraw, withhold, separate, and defend. Emotions are pure energy. It is how we perceive, identify with, and interpret them that cause us difficulty.

We *are* angry; not we *have* anger, but we *are* angry. I *am* furious; not I *have* rage. We totally identify with the feeling. We miss the message and become the medium. There is no space for us to move, because we have become the feeling.

"I'm in love," not I have love *for* so-and-so. By becoming the feeling, we become addicted to the highs and lows of the emotions. We must be "high" and if we can't, we seek it artificially. Then, when we aren't "high" on love—when the object of our love leaves or rejects us—we are devastated. We become "low." We *are* hurt, angry, frustrated. Then we fall in love again, and so on and on.

Emotions are great. Thank God for strong feelings—for contrast, depth, intensity, and duration. Thank God for the range of emotions and the nuances—for subtle feelings of change and discernment.

Emotions just *are*! They are not good or bad—they *are*. They provide the energy to fuel the act of creation. As the hands of God, how we use the gift of emotions determines the shape of the world. How we respond to that energy is the key. Can we look for the gift in strong emotion? Can we see the lesson in a situation that produces big feelings? Are we open to growing and learning with the language of emotion?

I used to be very closed to strong emotion. I was reared by a very controlled and controlling father, whose only emotional expression was to release anger. My mother was very emotionally withdrawn, non-supporting, and non-nurturing. I saw emotion as threat and weakness, a way of losing control. I saw no value in being emotional. It appeared to be weak, irrational, and nonsensical. I was afraid of emotion. As I mentioned before, I created great depressions because of these views.

Through a series of confrontations and insights, the lessons of feelings began to seep through. I saw the value of acknowledging and naming my fear. Just putting a name to it created some space between me and it. I could move and grow a little. It was all those unnamed fears and feelings, as well as the ones I could identify, that overwhelmed me.

So rather than *being* afraid, I *had* fear. This is a subtle distinction, but very important. By naming my fear and thus creating some detachment, I was able to start looking for the lessons in it. There were many.

It was a long, hard process of growth and discovery. I struggled with emotions (especially in relationships) for years. I still do. Occasional breakthroughs punctuating long spells of stunningly slow progress seem to be how I gain growth emotionally.

Then I discovered gratitude. What an amazing gift! I became able to feel blessed with having emotions. Each emotion became a beacon signaling the next lesson—the next gift!

I know for certain that the power of strong emotion lies in the gift it contains. Anger, fear, frustration are all hard to understand and decode the language, yet, when named, viewed with gratitude, and observed, the lesson and gift reveal themselves. Not all emotion must be expressed in order to gain the gift. Not all emotion needs to be named. Just an acknowledgment of the energy, and an awareness of its course, may be enough to receive its power.

I was having difficulty with one of my groups. For some reason, about half of the people were just not doing the exercises or "getting" the material. The other half were going gangbusters and growing by leaps and bounds. I became very frustrated with the group who wasn't doing the work.

I went home and named my emotions: I had frustration, I had anger with my frustration, and I had fear that under it all, I wasn't a good teacher and/or the material wasn't good. Just naming how I felt created some distance from it, and I started seeing more clearly.

The gifts in my feelings and the situation became apparent:

First, the resistance in the group (any group) was there for my benefit. It forced me to grow, to become a better teacher, a better server, a better giver.

Second, it let me see the inner resistance and work needed with myself. Anger and fear signaled the direction of my growth and awareness.

Third, a review of the material allowed me to simplify it, strengthen it, change the pace. The resistance of part of the group let me see new approaches and techniques.

By naming my emotions and by being grateful for the good in the situation, I learned a lot. An easy, open awareness of the energy and emotions allowed me to become open to the gift or message of their passage.

Take a situation that is bothering you and name the emotions. Now, underneath the emotions, name the gifts. Find the *value* in what you are feeling. Is it easy? *No.* If you are established in gratitude, stillness, and the use of the will, it can be. It takes time and practice. Do the irritations list exercise to develop the ability to detach and name emotions—even the subtle ones which disguise themselves and have different rationalizations. Invoke the power of the will in doing "will" statements to see the gifts in emotions. Practice meditation and gratitude to open to the stillness and majesty of the now.

In a surprisingly short period of time, the ability to detach from "hard" situations will be apparent, at least some of the time. Just practice—it will become easier and easier. With gratitude, it expands quickly.

By doing the irritations list exercises and the forgiveness work, some great changes take place. When we forgive ourselves and others, and become grateful for the love and grace of our Higher Self which allows us to do this, we begin to be better aligned with the qualities of the Higher Self. The more we practice gratitude and forgiveness, the more we identify with unconditional love. Each time we practice, meditate, or pray, we move closer into the embrace of God.

By seeing emotions as the soul's code, and being grateful, we short-cut the process. We become grateful and forgiveness is automatic. We no longer judge feelings as good or bad. We accept without conditions, demands, or expectations how we and others feel, and see the gift in the situation. We become whole and free. (See *The Next Step* for an in-depth discussion of emotions.)

 ## Emotion Worksheet

EXAMPLE:

Take the time to examine some of your current situations, such as:

	Situation	Name of Emotion	Gift
1.	Lack of job	Fear, anxiety, anger	Energy to keep looking.
2.	Relationship difficulty	Hurt, fear, anger	Motivation to get help. Energy to change. Willingness to grow.

Situation	Name of Emotion	Gift
1.		
2.		

Situation	Name of Emotion	Gift
3.		
4.		
5.		
6.		
7.		
8.		
9.		
10.		

Action

Love is the way I walk in gratitude.
—Gerald Jampolsky, M.D.

I finally understand gratitude. The exercises bring the truth about it home. Practice makes perfect and gratitude work is perfect practice.
—Workshop participant

Action is the way of gratitude. Without action, the gift has no meaning. God and the universe have made all the majesty and bounty, beauty and energy, creation and mystery, available to us. All the flow is ours, as we are the flow, *if we take action!*

For us to grow and become, to experience the flow and cleansing grace of God, there are two main acts we must perform. The first is invoking (deciding to use) the will. The second is sharing or giving (expressing love).

Making a decision is an act. Deciding sets the wheel in motion. Deciding to find a noble purpose, deciding to become grateful, deciding to *will* change in your life gets it all started. It is because we have a will that we can decide. God gave us a choice. We can move or not move. We can change or be passive. We can *be* whatever we choose to become.

It is through deciding that clarity and focus become reality. The act of deciding clears the decks for action and helps remove doubt, hesitancy, fear, and procrastination. The act of deciding is a spiritual act. There is more to it than an intellectual action. Deciding changes the nature of the now. What *is* will change. What *can be* will begin to become.

Decide! Choose! Will! To become more, have more, give more. Put your will behind a purpose and the gates of the universe open for you. With gratitude for the ability to choose, make a decision. Feel the power of the will drive you forward.

After honest effort and giving, if it is obvious that it is not working out, that it is a "bad" choice, then choose to change it. Don't let life happen to you, *make* it happen! *It is your choice.*

After deciding, after using the will, then it is time to *give*. Give your energy and effort wholeheartedly to the decision. Share the joy and satisfaction in moving, changing, becoming, and giving.

Give it all you've got. If you can't do that, then give what you can. A little effort leads to more effort. Giving is its own reward, and the universe gives back even more. By sharing or giving, discipline is developed. A little discipline, practiced daily, leads to more discipline. Through discipline, action becomes meaningful.

Sharing and giving are always rewarded: giving our full effort, dedication, resolve, intensity, and drive; giving our best—even if it is only a tiny piece of our best. Reap what you have sown, but *sow first*! Put out the energy. Give fully in the effort.

Share in the giving, the quiet joy and gratitude of being able to give full effort, the power of the will.

Share in the ability to decide and lead. Teach others how you've gained your ability to give. Teach gratitude and watch it expand. Teach action and watch self-esteem grow. Teach forgiveness and acceptance, and see serenity fill your life.

Share and give of the results of the effort. Detach from needing certain results. Will the effort and the giving and the results will take care of themselves. We have a tendency to become trapped and identify with the results. We give ourselves value based on results. If the results are good, we are successful. If the results are poor, we are failures. We want to be a "success," so unless we know we'll achieve successful results, we won't try. We are perfectionists, and since we know we rarely achieve perfection, we rarely try, especially if the results are in doubt.

Because of those views, many of us say, "I could have done that if I wanted to. I just didn't want to." We see someone else doing well, and we judge our insides by their outsides (results) and think we can't measure up, so we don't try. Or we become so identified with the results, with being a success, that we become a workaholic. We sacrifice all balance in order to achieve. "Winning" becomes everything, because if we don't win, we're losers.

How much simpler to realize that we can control our efforts, but we can't control the results! If we give full effort, expand in the process, the results will be what they will be, not a measure of who we are. Our *effort* is the measure of us. If we decide to try, and let go of the results, we gain just from the effort. A noble failure has in it as big a gift (or more) as an indifferent success.

The defeat at the Alamo has been told and retold many times for the lessons contained in it: the all-out effort; the bravery, heart, and sharing; the noble purpose and power of will, where a few could hold off overwhelming odds for so long. There are many examples in literature and history of the glorious and meaningful failures of those with a noble purpose. The purpose lived on and grew. How much better to *give* full effort and fail than never to try at all!

Action is the pulse of gratitude: give a little, gain a lot. Become more grateful. Give a little more, gain a lot more. Become more grateful. The cycle grows and expands.

The *practice* is the doing: doing the exercises, gratitude meditations, forgiveness. Meaning and experience are gained in the doing.

Belief, knowledge, and understanding add to the practice and give it depth and texture, but this works whether you believe, know, or understand it. All it requires is *action*, a little bit, a step at a time. You will *experience* the results and the process.

What a great gift God has given us. We gain satisfaction, joy, and fulfillment in the doing as well as in the gifts of the results. It makes us wonder why we hesitate at all, doesn't it?

Decide to keep growing and acting, and let the results take care of themselves.

 **Action Exercise #1**

Pick one area of your life that you'd like to improve. Determine one thing you can do (that you are not doing now) which would make a difference. For one week, *do it!* No holding back, no excuses, no limits. *Take action!*

**Area of
Improvement**   **Action**   **Difference**

 **Action Exercise #2**

Pick one of the exercises previously explained in this book—gratitude, irritation, deserve, or will. Make a decision to *take action*. Work the exercise you've chosen every night for one week, no excuses, no procrastinating. **Just do it!** After the week, notice any changes or differences in your life or attitude.

Exercise   **Action**   **Difference**

Action Exercise #3

For one week, either in the morning as part of your practice, or in the evening as part of your Step 10 inventory, do a forgiveness exercise. One night or morning, do a forgiveness of someone else. The next day, do a self-forgiveness. Every day for a week—do it!

Grace

*I am getting the **truth** that God provides the opportunity, through grace,
for joy, for duty, and for fulfillment.*
—*Workshop participant*

Grace allows us to take action even when we
don't have the ability to decide for ourselves. Grace is
God's gift as an instrument to strengthen the will when
it is incapacitated.

There are times when we are just not able to make
a decision—when we are not able to invoke the will:
when we are addicted, and acting out our addiction
(i.e., alcoholism, smoking, drugs, food, etc.), when we
are emotionally incapacitated, when we are physically
traumatized and in shock.

While we are acting out our addictions, it is almost
impossible to choose to stop. Grace intervenes and
makes it possible to stop, to get help, to accept help.
Grace makes it *possible*, for just an instant, to **see** the
addiction rather than **be** the addiction. Some of us
don't take advantage of grace. Others do. Most of the
time, our will is capable of pushing us to decision. Only
when we are incapacitated in some form does grace
play a part.

God provides grace to us all. It is a gift freely given.
God doesn't pick out individual drunks or addicts and

choose this one or that one to get sober or clean, and this one or that one to die in the gutter. He provides grace to them both, and the ultimate outcome is a result of their wills. To think otherwise is a grandiose exercise in self-importance. We are provided grace for those times when the gift of free will is diminished. Through grace, we are able to get or ask for help. If we choose not to ask, or not to take advantage of the help that is offered, it is our will at work, not God's.

It reminds me of the story of the man in the flood. His house was being flooded badly by a river, and it continued to rain. A sheriff came by in a four-by-four vehicle advising him to evacuate, that it appeared the flood would get worse. The man declined to leave, saying, "God will take care of me." The water continued to rise, and the man was forced to go to the second floor. From his bedroom window, he saw a boat approach, and the people in the boat offered to rescue him. He told them not to worry, go help someone else, "God will take care of me."

The water continued to rise. The man was forced onto his roof, holding onto the chimney. A rescue helicopter swung down to him, lowering a rescue sling. The man waved the helicopter off, shouting, "God will take care of me."

Soon after the helicopter left, the man lost his grip, was swept away by the flood, and drowned. When he arrived in heaven and approached God, he asked, "Why didn't You save me?" God replied, "I sent a truck, a boat, and a helicopter. What more could I do?"

Grace provides opportunity after opportunity for us to grow and change ourselves. If we do not use our will to take advantage of grace, it is a waste. It is certainly a futile exercise to blame God.

Gratitude enhances and reveals grace in all areas of our lives. If we are grateful, grace lubricates the wheels of our lives and everything goes smoother. Grace helps us in emotional situations. When we lose our detachment and gratitude, when we *are* the emotion, grace, again, allows us to *see* rather than *be* the emotion. We can then look for the gift in the situation and become grateful for it.

Grace is the buffer that gives us the space needed to move toward gratitude. We are *graceful* when we move in that space. Grace operates in our lives all the time. Normally, when we use the will in line with a noble purpose, grace smooths the way and helps all the processes flow together. One thing leads to another, automatically. In gratitude, we stay totally in the now with grace helping to show us the infinity of the moment, the unlimited choices and rewards.

Grace allows us to move into gratitude when we *can't* see the good, when all around us appears negative and hopeless and all within us appears poisoned and worthless. Grace gives us hope. It allows us to see that things can change. Grace shows us the will: that we have choices, that we can act, to give, to become, to have, which allows us to be grateful.

Grace is that quiet certainty that we are all children of God. It is the sure awareness underneath all the knowledge and belief and understanding. It is the thread of connectedness that assures us we are part of the flow—that we *are* the flow and it is us—no separation, no distance, no boundary.

Grace is a sureness that is underneath intuition and hunches, a knowing without knowledge. We can build our awareness of grace through gratitude. We must use the will to appreciate the glory of grace. It is a gift. As such, it is important to acknowledge it and be thankful for it.

 ## Grace Exercise

Take a few minutes to be quiet. Allow your breathing to slow and relax. Slow, easy breathing. Slow, easy mind. No grasping or holding. Just let your thoughts flow like a river. Now, think back to the last time you were aware of grace in your life. Remember how it felt to have grace operate in your life. Maybe it helped you make a hard decision. Maybe it let you be aware of choices. Perhaps it let you see people or opportunities in a way you hadn't before.

Take time to acknowledge and be grateful for grace in your life.

Accountability And Gratitude

*I've come to learn that through grati-
tude I've become accountable, and
therefore responsible for my own life. I
live in the now.*
                    —Workshop participant

Gratitude is the path that directly brings us to
God. To be more, become more, have more, give
more, gratitude gives us the way.

It is direct, simple, and powerful. All it takes is
action—a *little* action. Do the blessings list daily. Every
morning write out the list of those things you're grateful for. Become aware of all the good things in your life.
That leads to more awareness of the good. Gratitude
expands. As we become aware, there is *more* to be
aware of.

We choose to be grateful. Through will, we can
choose. To be able to choose also means accountability. If I have the power of choice, then I am responsible
for where I am today, and where I am going. (See *The
Next Step.*)

It is not circumstance. It is not my parents. It is not
where I was born or my education. It is because I *chose*
to be here. Most of us are not ready to face that. It

means we can't blame others or chance or the situation. We must face our choices. *We are accountable*.

It also means that, if it is our choice, we can change; we don't have to stay as we are or where we are. We can choose to make it different. Change may happen quickly or slowly. It may happen as we expect it and want it, or it may happen totally outside our expectations and beliefs, but it will happen if we make choices and take action.

I am accountable. It is not an act of God. God gave me choice. It is not some one else's fault. It is my choice. It is hard to face up to this, but in accepting accountability, we gain the power to change.

The current trend in our culture is to negate personal accountability. The eleven-year-old boy shot his sister because of television violence. It's not because his parents didn't shut the TV off. It's not because the father left the gun case unlocked. It's not because the boy chose to pull the trigger. It is violence on TV.

The thirty-five-year-old woman burned her daughter and broke her arm. It wasn't her fault. The mother was abused herself as a child, raised in a dysfunctional family. Her ex-husband was an alcoholic and beat her. It is not her fault, except she chose to take it out on the child. *She* did.

The forty-year-old man has been divorced twice. He has had lots of jobs with great futures. He never can seem to live up to his potential. He can never quite hold onto an intimate relationship. He has a way of creatively failing. But it is not his fault; he was raised in a dysfunctional family. His mother was an alcoholic. He never developed good self-esteem. He was warped by the experience. This is much more subtle, yet *it was his choice!*

To say otherwise is to say we have no control over the situation. If it is going to change, then we have to hope for circumstances to change. Well, I'm sorry, but that is not the case. We chose where we are today, and we can choose to change it. Through gratitude, grace, and the will, we can become more. What a fantastic gift! What an awesome responsibility!

As children, we of course are dependent on the choices of others, and those choices affect our whole lives, but to passively say that we can't change is to negate the gifts of will and grace. Reality is dealing with the situation as it is presented. Growth is seeing that the shape of reality can change. We are the instruments of that change.

I can hear you asking, "What makes this guy such an expert?" You'd have a legitimate question. What I have is accountability and experience. I've been given an awareness. I choose to share it, to give it away. It is my view; perhaps not a whole view and certainly not the only view. There is one destination, but many roads and paths. It doesn't matter which path we choose, as long as we *choose and take action*. Move toward God. He will move toward you.

When you do the exercises, and share the experience, then you will *know* how I can say what I say. If you just analyze, audit, and criticize, you will miss the impact of the message.

This is a tiny piece of the insight I've experienced. Some people will respond to it and will "know" intuitively the truth of the message. Some will resist it or even denounce it. The reason for that is that it calls for change. We can't experience this without change. We are accountable for the change. It can be a very hard concept to accept.

As I've said, this practice is about *doing*, not about understanding, knowing, or learning. The meaning becomes apparent through the doing. Choose to do it.

Be accountable. Be grateful. We can change. We've been given the gift of choice, of using our will to make things different. Being accountable is not just a general feeling. It is specific. How much more am I giving in money, time, and effort than I was? Where, specifically, are my priorities? How could someone who doesn't know me tell what my priorities are? How much each month am I giving to charity? How much more each month am I saving? How much more time each month am I giving as a volunteer? How much time each day have I set aside for my exercises?

Being accountable means doing the exercises every day, *no matter what*, and knowing that each day that I *don't* do the exercises is a choice to move away from gratitude. You have the choice to move in any direction. By choosing the path of gratitude, it will all become available to you: all the possibilities, potential, and grace. *It is your choice*.

Accountability Exercise

Make a list of those areas in your life where you haven't always chosen to be accountable. It could be relationships, or a tendency to blame others for your problems. It might be work, blaming the boss or the economy or lack of opportunity for where you are, rather than being personally accountable. What other areas in your life have you let slide?

Take one of those areas and *choose* to be totally accountable for one month. You are responsible and accountable for *everything* in that area of your life for one month, no blaming, no excuses, no rationalizing. Just accept and do what you can.

Choose to give it a legitimate effort. Then take a look at it. Where are you now and where were you 30 days ago? Now *decide* what to do.

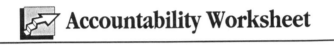 **Accountability Worksheet**

Area   **Difference**   **Decision**

Area   **Difference**   **Decision**

Blessings

> *I'm hooked. I don't understand it, but through gratitude, through will, through forgiveness, my whole life is different. I'm much more unconditional, present, and accepting.*
>
> *—Workshop participant*

I *am grateful for the blessings in my life.* For breath and air, expansion and contraction, for sense of passage.

I am grateful for my body. For the height and weight of it, for the miraculous functioning of it, the amazing grace of it, and the fullness of it. The prime of it and the illness. The pleasure and the pain, the appetites and hungers, the satiation and fulfillments.

I am grateful for mind. For speculation, imagination, and fantasy. For dreaming and playing. For learning and knowledge, deduction and reason, for understanding and awareness. For potential and openness. For belief and bias. For knowing and not knowing.

I am grateful for family. For love and acceptance. For forming and bonding. For belief and value. For ability and talent. For potential and function. For relationship and style. I am grateful for pain and betrayal. For abuse and denial. For survival and strength. For rigidity and compulsion. For pushing, in order for me to resist. For continuing to be in order for me to become. For awareness of growth and change. For contrast and comparison.

I am grateful for friends. For differences and sameness. For loyalty and caring. For acceptance and sharing. For companionship and fellowship. For trust, and the breaking of trust. For change and growth. For going away and coming back. For lessons of faith and failure, joy and pain.

I am grateful for relationships. For sharing and caring. For creating and expanding. For ecstasy and intimacy. For respect and honor. For forging and polishing. For loving and forgiving. For passion and intensity. For longing and aching need. For doubt and fear. For hurt and tenderness. For reassurance and rejection.

I am grateful for experiences. For all those that made me stronger, that pushed me to becoming more and being more, that tested me. For all those that taught me tenderness and gentleness. For all those that taught me fortitude and perseverance. For all those that taught me how to handle pain and loneliness. For all those that made me face belief and bias and prejudice. For all those that reaffirmed faith and hope and optimism.

I am grateful for all the good teachers who gave to me, and all the bad teachers who still taught me.

I am grateful for senses. For the beauty of nature and sunsets and sunrises. For beautiful poetry and music. For flower and bee. For humming and laughter. For light and dark. For contrast. For clarity and focus. For purpose and resolve. For giving and receiving. For possibility. For richness and depth. For experience. For the flow. For gratitude.

Thank you, God, for the richness and variety of this existence.

And thank *you*, dear reader, for your energy and patience. I know you will have gained a new view, a different approach, if you have tried the exercises. I hope you have and will. Give full effort in your endeavors. Live with purpose. Live with gratitude.

Thanks,

Todd

Photo by Andy

About the Author

Todd Weber is a Ph.D. candidate in Psychology. He maintains a private counseling practice in the Seattle area, where he also instructs at community colleges, and teaches workshops throughout the Northwest. Todd consults for a number of recovery centers and teaches continuing education for professionals dealing with recovery issues.

For information on workshops, tapes, or seminars:

Todd A. Weber
P.O. Box 3225
Kirkland, WA 98083

Inquiries, orders, and requests for
catalogs and discount schedules
should be addressed to:

Glen Abbey Books, Inc.
P.O. Box 31329
Seattle, Washington 98103

Toll-free 24-hour
Order and Information Line
1-800-782-2239
(All U.S.)